HOLY DAYS

Sally Nemeth

BROADWAY PLAY PUBLISHING INC
224 E 62nd St, NY NY 10065-8201
212 772-8334 fax: 212 772-8358
BroadwayPlayPubl.com

HOLY DAYS
© Copyright 1991 by Sally Nemeth

First published by B P P I in August 1991
First printing, this edition: May 2012
I S B N: 978-0-88145-522-9

Book design: Marie Donovan
Page make-up: Adobe Indesign
Typeface: Palatino
Printed and bound in the U S A

ABOUT THE AUTHOR

Sally Nemeth is an award winning playwright and screenwriter. Her plays have been produced by theaters throughout the English speaking world. Other published plays include MILL FIRE, WATER PLAY and SALLY'S SHORTS. Since beginning her television career writing for the hit N B C show *Law & Order*, she has written for every major television network, and produced the documentary *Long Story Short*. Her novel for young adults, *The Heights, the Depths and Everything in Between*, is published by Knopf/Yearling. You can visit her at www.sallynemeth.com.

HOLY DAYS premiered in London England on 16 March 1988. It was produced by the Soho Poly Theater (Sue Dunderdale, Artistic Director; Annette Clancy, Administrative Director) in association with Alexander E and Dina Racolin. The cast and creative contributors were as follows:

ROSIE .... Brid Brennan
GANT .... Brian Protheroe
WILL .... David Beames
MOLLY .... Barbara Barnes

Director .... Brian Stirner
Set design .... Michael Taylor
Lighting design .... Rick Fisher
Costumes .... Katie Birell
Production manager .... Dennis Charles
Stage manager .... Danielle Bisson
Assistant stage managers .... Amanda George
& Graham Oulds

HOLY DAYS premiered in the U S at South Coast
Repertory in Costa Mesa, California on 26 January
1990. The cast and creative contributors were as
follows:

ROSIE..Jeanne Paulsen
GANT .... Richard Doyle
WILL..John K Linton
MOLLY ....Devon Raymond

Director...Martin Benson
Set design...John Iacovelli
Lighting design.. Tom Ruzika
Costumes...Ann Bruice
Music & sound .... Michael Roth
Production manager .... Paul Hammond
Stage manager..Andy Tighe
Assistant stage manager ....Christine Santmyers

CHARACTERS & SETTING

ROSIE, GANT's *wife, age thirty-five*
GANT, WILL's *brother, age thirty-seven*
WILL, *age thirty-five*
MOLLY, WILL's *wife, age twenty-six*

The action of the play takes place in ROSIE *and* GANT's
kitchen. WILL *and* MOLLY's *farmhouse is adjacent to* ROSIE
and GANT's *house. The farm is in western Kansas. The time
of the play is Good Friday to Easter Sunday, 1936.*

(Scene: 1936, western Kansas, Good Friday. ROSIE *stands outside the back screen door, scanning the horizon.* ROSIE *is wearing a cotton dress with a cardigan over it. It is a little past lunchtime, and a small dust storm has just cleared.)*

ROSIE: There was a time I recall when things was just beginning to come green all around. My daffodils come up early. Then it snowed—not heavy, but enough to make me certain they'd gone. And I went out to cut the flowers that already opened. If I couldn't have daffodils out front of the house, I'd sure have them all over inside. Anyway, I went out with my shears and all of them had opened—they was sitting in snow and they was open as you please. I started cutting at them, and it seemed I'd brought in armfuls and there was still more to cut. Almost like they was opening before my eyes. Opening and growing all around me. I didn't have but one or two pitchers, so I left them be and went back inside to put the ones I'd cut in water. I swear I'd brought in enough to cover the table, but all it came out to be was barely a pitcher full. Well, I went back out to cut more, but there weren't no more to cut. I'd just seen them out there—dozens of yellow flowers in the snow—now there weren't none. And the stems and leaves was all black—not like they'd frozen, but— dry. Dry as a bone.

*(*ROSIE *turns and enters the kitchen. There is a table with six chairs in the middle of the kitchen. A large wood stove occupies one wall; sink and cabinets take up another. There is a back screen door near the stove and a window over the sink. A hallway leads to the rest of the house. There is an*

icebox and a door to the pantry. A cloth covers a completely set and laid-out table. Dust covers the cloth and everything in the room. ROSIE *picks up a rag and slaps it on her thigh to knock the dust out of it. She takes the rag and ties it over her nose and mouth, picks up a broom, and starts to clear the dust off the chairs, then begins to sweep.)*

(GANT *and* WILL *enter from the screen door.* GANT *is* WILL*'s older brother and is* ROSIE*'s husband. Both are dusty and are wearing hats and rags over their faces. They turn as they enter, go out to the steps, and knock some of the dust off themselves. They re-enter.)*

ROSIE: Doesn't much matter. You weren't going to make it any dirtier than it already is.

GANT: I suppose.

ROSIE: Thought you'd be later with the blow and all.

GANT: We saw it coming before it hit. Got part way home before it met us.

WILL: Just a little blow anyway. Didn't last.

(ROSIE *starts to fold the cloth over the table in on itself to keep it from spilling dust on the food.)*

GANT: Let me help.

ROSIE: I got it. You'll just spill it.

(GANT *and* WILL *sit down at the table. Bread, chicken meat, butter, milk, and some potato salad are laid out.* ROSIE *takes the cloth to the door to shake it out.)*

ROSIE: I'm sorry it's all cold food but I didn't know how long it would storm and I didn't want to be cooking.

WILL: This is fine. Just fine. (*He removes his hat.)*

ROSIE: I know Molly usually makes a hot lunch. (*She sits at the table.)*

WILL: When we get caught out there it just gets cold anyway. This is just fine.

GANT: Molly should have been back by now, shouldn't she?

WILL: No. You know she's always back late. She has to wait at the doctor's office, then she usually takes her sweet time, looking at store windows and all.

ROSIE: She loves to shop.

WILL: I know it. If we had any money we wouldn't have any money.

ROSIE: No worse off than when you started.

WILL: That's right.

GANT: Aren't you eating anything, Rosie?

ROSIE: No. I'm not very hungry.

GANT: You ought to eat something.

ROSIE: I had a little something when I was fixing it.

GANT: I wish you wouldn't do that. I always feel funny eating when there's someone at the table who isn't eating.

ROSIE: Well, Gant, then I'll just go find something to do. (*Starts to rise*)

GANT: Sit down, Rosie. Come on. I didn't mean for you to leave. I just wish you'd eat with us.

ROSIE: I do have things to do.

GANT: They can wait until lunch is over.

WILL: Your wash out on the line ain't going to get any dirtier.

ROSIE: Oh no. I forgot it was out there.

WILL: You probably didn't have time to bring it in.

ROSIE: No, I had the time. I just forgot. Now I'm going to have to do every bit of it again. I don't know what I was thinking about. *(Rises and gets the laundry basket by the door and heads out)*

GANT: Rosie—it can wait!

WILL: Sorry. I wouldn't have mentioned it.

GANT: I figured she knew about it, too.

(MOLLY enters from the hallway door. She is about seven months pregnant. She looks tired and bedraggled.)

WILL: *(Stands and kisses her)* Honey, I didn't even hear you pull up.

MOLLY: *(Sits and puts her feet up on a chair)* That's because I didn't.

WILL: What happened?

MOLLY: I pulled off when the dust started to blow—decided I'd sit it out instead of trying to drive through it. Well, when I went to start the truck again—nothing. Wouldn't start for nothing. So this nice man pulls over and tries to start it and he can't get it started. So, he give me a ride to the driveway and I walked from there.

WILL: You should have had him take you to the door. That's like a half- mile from the mailbox to the door.

MOLLY: He was nice enough to bring me as far as he did. Anyway, I didn't think he'd make it. He was in a little two-seater and I knew for sure it would never make it over the wheel ruts.

WILL: You rode in a two-seater?

MOLLY: Yes, I did. With California plates.

GANT: I'd have loved to see you get out of it.

MOLLY: I required a lot of help.

GANT: How far away is the truck?

MOLLY: About halfway between here and town.

WILL: Why didn't you go back into town and get someone from the gas station out to help you?

MOLLY: The man wasn't going that way. Besides, gas station's closed.

WILL: Closed? Why? Someone die or something?

GANT: Well, yeah, sort of—

MOLLY: Gant—don't you dare. (*Pause*) It's Good Friday, Will, remember?

WILL: Oh, yeah. Right.

MOLLY: Heathens.

GANT: Was the doctor open?

MOLLY: Of course.

WILL: How are we doing?

MOLLY: We're all doing just fine, thank you. And we all may be doing even better very soon.

WILL: How's that?

MOLLY: Well, while I was waiting for the doctor, one of the men working down on the railroad smashed up his hand real bad and one of his buddies brought him in. I sat out there and passed the time with this man's buddy. Joe was his name, and he told me the Santa Fe is going to hire a whole bunch of men through the W P A to build a bridge over the Cimmarron River Valley.

WILL: We should head down to the railroad office. Head down there right away.

GANT: Santa Fe's hiring through the W P A?

MOLLY: That's what the man said.

GANT: Then all we got to do is stay put. We're both registered with the W P A. There's any work and they'll let us know.

MOLLY: That ain't so. Joe said you got to be there when they start hiring.

GANT: Molly, that can't be right. That's not how they do things.

MOLLY: Right or not, that's what the man told me.

WILL: We should still go see.

MOLLY: Never hurts to check up on these things.

GANT: We got to go get the truck, anyway. All right— we'll take the tractor to the truck and then I'll go ahead and take the truck into town.

WILL: I hope the W P A's open—you know, if the gas station's closed—

GANT: They can't be closed—it's a government office.

MOLLY: Don't be too sure.

GANT: You were in town, Molly—couldn't you have found out?

MOLLY: It sounded to me like you just had to show up when they were hiring.

GANT: And when's that?

MOLLY: I don't know. All I know is what I already told you.

WILL: It can't hurt to try. The loan 's due soon and we need some cash.

MOLLY: That's for sure.

WILL: And a W P A job is the only cash around.

GANT: Sounds like a lot of nothing to me, but I'll go check on it.

WILL: I'll go into town if you don't want to.

GANT: It's not that I don't want to. It's just that I don't really think there's any reason to.

MOLLY: Sounds like a real long-term job. Building a bridge.

GANT: Those things usually are.

MOLLY: Well, if there is some work it could mean a good deal of time away from the farm.

GANT: Molly, neither Will or I are heading off to build any bridges yet, so let's not worry about that, all right?

MOLLY: Just thinking out loud. *(Pause)* Where's Rosie?

WILL: Taking her wash off the line.

MOLLY: *(Gets up and goes to the door)* Gant, she's just standing there with the basket in her arms.

GANT: *(Joins MOLLY at the door)* Oh, no. *(Goes out the door)*

MOLLY: She been out there long?

WILL: As long as you've been here.

MOLLY: Her wash is still all out on the line.

WILL: Come here and sit down. Gant will take care of her.

MOLLY: I should go out and help her.

WILL: Leave them alone for a bit. She gets embarrassed when you do things for her.

MOLLY: I know, but when is she going to start doing things for herself again? *(She sits next to him.)*

WILL: I don't know.

MOLLY: I don't mean to be mean or anything. I don't mind doing for her. I just know she doesn't like it. She doesn't like to be this way.

WILL: I don't know anyone that would.

MOLLY: Another couple months and I won't have the time to help her out as much.

WILL: By that time I'm sure she'll be helping you. It'll make her feel good to have a baby around.

MOLLY: I'm not so sure about that.

WILL: What do you mean?

MOLLY: Nothing. I just hope the baby's a girl. I think having a little girl would be the best thing, don't you?

WILL: A girl would be all right.

MOLLY: Well, I think it would be nice. Come on. You can still play catch with a girl.

WILL: But I'll never teach her to throw.

MOLLY: I can throw.

WILL: You throw like a girl.

MOLLY: I do not.

WILL: Do too.

MOLLY: I was the best pitcher the Methodists ever had.

WILL: So, you threw better than the rest of the girls. But you still throw like a girl.

MOLLY: Five cents says I can strike you out.

(GANT and ROSIE enter, GANT carrying the laundry.)

MOLLY: Hey, Rosie.

ROSIE: Hello. You get caught in the storm?

MOLLY: Sure did. Sat it out in the truck. Then the truck wouldn't start, so I got a ride back here.

GANT: We need to get to that truck.

ROSIE: Did the doctor say everything's all right?

MOLLY: Yes. I checked out all right.

WILL: Why don't I pull the tractor around and you go get some tools.

GANT: What did the truck sound like when you tried to start it?

MOLLY: Not much. It would turn some but it wouldn't catch.

GANT: I bet it's just clogged with dust.

MOLLY: I'd have no idea.

GANT: I'll bring all the tools, anyway. Let's go, Will.

WILL: See you at dinner, ladies.

(WILL *kisses* MOLLY *on top of her head, and they exit.* ROSIE *starts to clear the table, then stops.*)

ROSIE: I'm sorry. You have any lunch yet?

MOLLY: No, I haven't. I'll just fix myself a sandwich here. You leave it all out, I'll put it away when I'm done.

ROSIE: All right. (*She continues to clear dirty plates from the table.*)

MOLLY: Rosie, just leave it.

ROSIE: I'm only clearing what's dirty. Let me do that much. (*She continues to clear and sets the dishes in the sink but does not rinse them.*)

MOLLY: You collect eggs yet today?

ROSIE: No, there was a storm. I couldn't see the coop from here.

MOLLY: Must've blown worse here than where I was. I had trouble seeing but it wasn't that thick.

ROSIE: I really couldn't see it.

MOLLY: I don't doubt it.

ROSIE: Anyway, the hens get so scared when it blows like that they don't lay many eggs.

MOLLY: They better have laid some. I want to color some eggs.

ROSIE: It's Easter already?

MOLLY: On Sunday.

ROSIE: I thought it was another week or so. I didn't even make any plans for supper. What are we going to have?

MOLLY: I don't know. I haven't given it much thought either.

ROSIE: We have to have an Easter supper. We can all go to church with you in the morning.

MOLLY: You're more than welcome to join me, but I know you'll never get Gant or Will anywhere near a church.

ROSIE: I know. Well, whatever they want to do, but we're going to have an Easter supper. Oh, I don't even know what we have in the pantry.

MOLLY: Nothing exciting, but enough for a respectable meal.

ROSIE: We've got a hundred things to do. Baking pies and things and...

MOLLY: (Pause) We've got time to do it all. You want to invite anyone over to join us?

ROSIE: No. I don't know who I'd ask.

MOLLY: Probably just as well. Short notice and all.

ROSIE: Well, I've got to re-do my wash. It got caught out in the storm. I didn't have time to go out and get it. (Goes to door and picks up basket) I think having an Easter supper will be nice, don't you?

MOLLY: It'll be real nice.

(ROSIE exits.)

(While MOLLY delivers the next speech, she clears the table. There will be a shift of time during the speech, and when she is through, it will be evening.)

MOLLY: It never occurred to us to leave. We'd all heard of people who did go only to find that things were tough all over. This was our home—it had been passed on to Will and Gant by their folks to keep as it had been kept before, and when things were good they were very good. When everyone's land was full of wheat I can't think of anything more beautiful. Far as you could see, the wind would make waves through the wheat and you could fool yourself and play like your house was a ship on the ocean and you were on your way to China or somewhere. That was a favorite game of his. A Sunday afternoon game. Barbary pirates on the high seas. We got very elaborate. I made him an eye patch and Gant or Will, I don't remember, made swords from some old lumber. Then he got it in his mind that he wanted a parrot. All the pirates in the books had parrots. Aren't many parrots in this part of the world. (*She should be finished clearing the table. She takes a deck of cards out of a drawer of the table. The lights dim. It is evening, after dinner. She sits and shuffles the deck.*) Will! You done with that cigarette yet?

WILL: (*From outside*) Just about.

MOLLY: I'm tired of playing solitaire.

WILL: (*Grinding out cigarette with heel*) You wouldn't have to play solitaire if you'd let me smoke inside.

MOLLY: You know that ever since I've been pregnant the smell makes me sick.

WILL: You got sick once and that was a long time ago.

MOLLY: Better safe than sorry. You know how much I hate throwing up.

WILL: I don't know anyone that enjoys it.

ROSIE: (*Entering from hallway*) Enjoys what?

WILL: Throwing up.

ROSIE: Why are you talking about that?

MOLLY: Will's tired of smoking outside, but I won't let him smoke inside because since I've been pregnant it makes me sick.

WILL: Once.

MOLLY: It still makes me sick.

ROSIE: Sometimes I think feeling sick and queasy is worse than actually getting sick.

WILL: I can think of a couple instances when I was happy to get sick.

MOLLY: I'm sure you can.

ROSIE: I was sick the whole time I was pregnant.

MOLLY: Don't tell me that.

ROSIE: Everybody told me something different about when it would end, but it never did.

MOLLY: I've heard all sorts of things. Everybody's got an opinion and a remedy.

WILL: You going to deal those cards or are you going to let us watch you cheat at solitaire?

MOLLY: I was waiting for Gant.

WILL: He'll be back any time now.

ROSIE: Maybe the truck's broke down again.

WILL: We got it started right up. He probably just ran into some people in town.

ROSIE: That's not like him.

WILL: Maybe not, but I'll bet that's what happened.

MOLLY: What do you want me to deal?

WILL: How about seven-card stud?

MOLLY: Will—

WILL: All right then. Five-card draw.

MOLLY: *(Hands him deck)* You deal.

WILL: *(To MOLLY)* You'll play?

MOLLY: How about it, Rosie?

ROSIE: You'll have to remind me of the game.

WILL: All right. *(Shuffles the deck)* Could you get the matches off the stove?

(ROSIE goes to the stove.)

WILL: Both boxes.

(ROSIE returns with them and sits.)

WILL: O K. The red tips are five cents and the blue tips are ten. You get five cards face down. You bet on them. You get to discard up to three and get new ones from me, your dealer, and then you bet on that hand. Then we show hands and the winner takes the pot.

ROSIE: What beats what? I can never remember.

MOLLY: Royal flush beats flush beats four-of-a-kind beats straight beats, uh, don't tell me—full house? Full house beats three-of-a-kind, no, two pairs beats three-of-a-kind beats a pair. Right?

WILL: *(Shuffling)* Something like that.

MOLLY: I'll help you with your first couple hands.

WILL: Cut the deck. *(Sets the deck in front of ROSIE and she cuts.)* Take some matches, ladies, and ante up.

MOLLY: I'd forgot about this part.

WILL: Pay to play, pay to play.

MOLLY: All right, fine, deal the cards.

(They all ante. WILL deals the cards and MOLLY counts along to herself as he deals. When the cards are dealt and the hands picked up, GANT enters.)

ROSIE: Gant. Where have you been?

GANT: In town.

WILL: Sorry, this hand's dealt. You'll have to wait until the next to get in the game.

GANT: What are you playing?

MOLLY: Five-card draw.

GANT: You're kidding.

ROSIE: Why don't you take my hand, Gant? I'll get your dinner out of the oven.

GANT: No, Rosie. I want to see you play this.

ROSIE: I have no idea what I'm doing.

GANT: Then it's a good thing you're playing for matches.

WILL: How many you want?

ROSIE: I don't know.

WILL: It's Molly's turn.

MOLLY: I'm not ready yet.

WILL: Well, it's still your turn.

MOLLY: Aren't we supposed to bet first?

GANT: None of you have any idea what you're doing.

WILL: Gant, I knew that.

GANT: Then, how come you asked her how many she wanted before you found out how much she was spending?

MOLLY: I'll bet five cents.

GANT: Match the bet, Rosie.

ROSIE: I'll match.

WILL: I'll meet that and raise it a nickel.

MOLLY: Call.

GANT: Call.

ROSIE: Call.

MOLLY: I'll take three cards.

WILL: *(Dealing out)* There you go. Rosie?

ROSIE: *(Points out a card in her hand to* GANT. *He nods.)* One.

WILL: There's some daring. And the dealer takes three.

ROSIE: Well, I didn't get anything. *(Lays down her hand)*

GANT: Rosie, you still could have bet on it.

ROSIE: I know that, but I don't feel like betting on nothing.

WILL: Smart lady. Molly?

MOLLY: What?

ROSIE: I'll get your dinner.

WILL: Bet.

GANT: Just sit. It'll wait.

MOLLY: I'll bet a dime.

WILL: A dime? I'll call that and raise you a quarter.

MOLLY: I'll call that.

GANT: Let's see the cards, Molly.

MOLLY: Full house.

GANT: Sure is. Jacks high. Will?

WILL: There you go. *(Lays hand down)*

GANT: Pair of eights?

MOLLY: *(Raking in pile)* It's a good thing you're playing for matches.

WILL: How's the truck?

GANT: Truck's fine.

WILL: Sounded pretty good after we got it going.

ROSIE: Why did you go into town if you got it started yourself?

WILL: Gant wanted to—

GANT: It hasn't been looked at in a while. Just making sure.

MOLLY: I want to play another hand. That was fun.

ROSIE: So what took you so long in town?

GANT: Oh, you know. Ran into some people in town. Hadn't seen them in a while.

WILL: What's the news?

GANT: The usual. Some rumors about a W P A job with the Santa Fe. Building a bridge in the Cimmarron River Valley.

MOLLY: Just rumors?

GANT: No. This one seems to be happening. I went over to the W P A office.

ROSIE: I don't know how they expect farmers to work W P A. When you leave to go work for them you aren't doing anything for your land.

GANT: What land, Rosie? All our topsoil is probably halfway across the country by now.

ROSIE: So what are you and Will doing out there on the tractor every day? You know you have to work it to keep it all from going.

GANT: I'm not so sure I know that anymore.

WILL: Bad time of year for them to be taking people from the farms.

MOLLY: When are they going to build, Will, in the winter?

WILL: There's never a good time, but—

ROSIE: I think it's ridiculous. Trying to hire people out when they know people are planting. *(Gets up to get plate out of oven)* I'm sure this plate of food is all dried out from being in the oven too long.

GANT: It's all right, Rosie.

ROSIE: Oh, it is. It's all dried out. You want me to scramble you some eggs?

GANT: No. I got some dinner in town.

ROSIE: You shouldn't have done that. You know I always keep a plate for you.

GANT: Rosie, I signed up.

ROSIE: *(Puts plate on stove)* No.

GANT: Yes, Rosie. I had to.

ROSIE: No.

GANT: If we have a summer like the last one we'll never make our loan. I got to make the cash.

(MOLLY *lights a match and watches it burn, then blows it out.)*

GANT: Rosie?

(ROSIE *leaves, running up the hall.)*

GANT: Oh, damn.

MOLLY: It's better you let her know right away so she has time to get used to it.

GANT: Ain't no time. I leave Sunday.

MOLLY: Sunday?

GANT: Even if she had time it wouldn't be any easier. *(He exits hallway.)*

MOLLY: Come on. Let's go home.

WILL: I'm going to stay for a minute. I want to talk to Gant.

MOLLY: About what?

WILL: I just want to talk with him.

MOLLY: If you think you're going to talk him into letting you go instead, you're wrong. I ain't having this baby alone.

WILL: Go on. I'll be home in a little bit.

MOLLY: Will—

WILL: Don't worry. I think he's half-relieved to be going.

MOLLY: That's a terrible thing to say.

WILL: That doesn't change the fact that it's true.

MOLLY: No, it doesn't. Don't be too long.

WILL: I won't.

(MOLLY *exits screen door.* WILL *shuffles cards and deals himself solitaire.* GANT *re-enters hallway door.*)

GANT: You still here?

WILL: I didn't guess she'd feel much like conversation.

GANT: (*Goes to sink, gets a tin from under the sink. Opens it and takes out a pint bottle of whisky.*) Join me?

WILL: Molly will smell that on me a mile away.

GANT: (*Takes a swig*) So?

WILL: (*Laughs*) Right. (*Reaches for bottle and drinks*) How long have you had that hid?

GANT: I don't know.

WILL: If I even thought about having a bottle in the house, Molly would know where I was thinking about hiding it.

GANT: This bottle could have sat on the stove and I don't think Rosie would have even noticed it.

WILL: She's seemed better to me.

GANT: Maybe. I can't tell.

WILL: She was having fun playing poker and all.

GANT: She was?

WILL: You saw her.

GANT: All I saw was her fussing about my dinner.

WILL: No, she was having fun.

GANT: And then I came home.

WILL: Gant, you know that's not—

GANT: Just as well I'm going. I don't feel like I'm doing any good here one way or the other.

WILL: That ain't true.

GANT: Come on. We go out there every day trying to put something in the ground to just hold it down—and nothing. For nothing.

WILL: We haven't had as bad luck as some of the others.

GANT: You seen anything grow out there in a while? Have you?

WILL: Gant, this ain't just rough on you.

GANT: Far as I can tell it's going to be a good deal rougher on you.

WILL: What do you mean?

GANT: Whole farm—what's left of it—and just you to take care of it. (Takes a swig) Seems hardly worth hanging on at times, don't it?

WILL: I'm not sure what you're getting at, but I ain't selling out for nothing and hitting the road like those poor stupid sons-of-bitches—everything but the cow tied onto their car.

GANT: Hold on.

WILL: You know you can't sell without my O K.

GANT: I've said nothing about selling.

WILL: Then what the hell are you saying?

GANT: *(Takes a drink)* You've got a baby on the way. I'd never think of putting you on the road.

(GANT offers the bottle; WILL drinks.)

GANT: I may not be the one to put you there.

WILL: Oh?

GANT: I don't know if this job's going to make us enough money, that's just it.

WILL: Any money is more than we got.

GANT: I'll tell you, they say they got close to three years of work out there. That's a long time for you to be the only one here, but I'll work as long as you need me to and I'll make us some money.

WILL: You won't have to work any three years. Some money will do us. They'll take part of a loan payment in good faith.

GANT: We'll see.

WILL: The money you send us will make us more money, too—I'll see to that. Weather won't be bad forever, you know. You'll be back here sooner than you know it.

GANT: *(Takes a swig)* You want any more?

WILL: No. Yeah. One more. *(Takes a drink)*

GANT: *(Closes bottle and returns it to its hiding place)* Bedtime.

WILL: Yeah. *(Stands and stretches)* You got anything to take this whisky off my breath?

GANT: Try brushing your teeth.

WILL: I mean before I go home.

GANT: Go on home, Will. What's she going to do, shoot you?

WILL: It's your fault if she does. Goodnight. *(Exits screen door)*

(GANT watches him leave, then retrieves the bottle from its hiding place. He drinks as he speaks to us, leaning on the sink, then sitting at the table. When the speech is done it will be Saturday morning.)

GANT: When I'm on the tractor and the land starts to blow—that's when it comes back the hardest. Can't hear nothing but the wind in my ears. Can't even hear the tractor running, not even sure that it's moving, as I can't see but a yard in front of me. Then, the dust fills my ears and eyes and clogs the rag tied over my nose and mouth. And time stops. I can't be sure if I've been in the blow five minutes or five hours. Just can't tell. And that's when he comes to me the clearest. Trying to get home from the school. Sure he's on the right path, but not sure how much farther. Times I think I see him myself, and come close to jumping off the tractor to lead him the rest of the way. It's not far. Not too much more. There's two of us. Two of us won't get lost. I come back to, crawling off my tractor seat and know the tricks the storm can play. It ain't settled with him—it wants me, too. And it has crossed my mind how easy it would be to let it have what it wants. Easy as stepping off the tractor and setting my feet on the wind.

(GANT puts his head on his folded arms and sleeps as morning comes.)

(Saturday A M—GANT asleep on kitchen table, head on arms. The bottle is in front of him. MOLLY enters from screen door, sees GANT, and keeps the door from slamming, closing it gently. She carries a bowl of hard-boiled eggs with her. She sets the eggs silently on the table, picks up the bottle

and looks at it. She carries the bottle over to the sink, dumps the contents, brings the bottle back to the table and puts it down loudly. GANT *jumps, then rubs his face.*)

GANT: Rosie, I'll be to—

MOLLY: It's morning, Gant.

GANT: *(Sitting up quickly)* Molly. Oooohf. *(Realizing how stiff he is, he rubs his back.)*

MOLLY: Stiff?

GANT: Yeah.

MOLLY: Serves you right.

GANT: *(Sees the bottle in front of him and looks up at her)* I didn't drink that whole thing.

MOLLY: I know, Will helped you.

GANT: *(Picks it up)* No. There was some left.

MOLLY: Well, there isn't now.

GANT: *(Sets bottle down, stands and stretches)* What time is it?

MOLLY: Close to seven.

GANT: I wonder why Rosie didn't wake me up.

MOLLY: Probably because she's not up.

GANT: She's always up at the crack of dawn.

MOLLY: So are you.

GANT: *(Goes to icebox and gets a pitcher of water)* You've made your point, Molly. *(Pours a glass)* I drank some whisky last night. So did Will. I know you think we do it just to annoy you, but I promise that wasn't on our minds at all. *(Drinks some water)*

MOLLY: There's no need to be so cross.

GANT: There's no need to pour half a bottle of perfectly good whisky down the sink. (*Pours the rest of the glass of water over his head, leaning over sink. Rubs his face*)

MOLLY: I did no such thing.

GANT: Righteous people make rotten liars, Molly. (*Pours another glass of water*) Where's Will?

MOLLY: He's messing with the cow. She's got no milk.

GANT: She ain't been steady for a while. Got nothing decent to feed her.

MOLLY: We'll have to get something. I won't be able to do without her.

GANT: We sure as hell won't get another feed and seed loan. Not until we make good on the last one.

MOLLY: You know what the pay schedule on this railroad job is?

GANT: Every two weeks. They'll hold the first check two weeks, though. It'll be a month before we see any money.

MOLLY: We can keep her alive for a month. But she may go dry completely.

GANT: Then just keep her alive and get some issue powdered milk in the meantime.

MOLLY: I hate to do that.

GANT: You've got it coming. It's paid for.

MOLLY: I just hate to start taking things that other people probably need more. We've done all right.

GANT: You ain't taking nothing that we didn't pay for. That's why we pay taxes—so when we can't afford things the government can. And there's a hell of a lot of things we can't afford right now. For starters, we can't afford to feel like a charity case.

MOLLY: I don't feel like a charity case.

GANT: I do. (*Gulps down the rest of his water*) I'm going to find Will. We've got a lot to do before I leave tomorrow.

MOLLY: When exactly are you leaving?

GANT: Morning.

MOLLY: Morning? It's Easter Sunday.

GANT: I got to be at the railroad office in the valley Monday morning and Will's got to get me to a line that connects there.

MOLLY: Can't it wait until evening?

GANT: I don't know when the line runs and I don't want to chance missing it.

MOLLY: I can't believe they'd have you travel on Easter.

GANT: They don't care what day it is. It really don't matter to me either. The job starts on Monday. I'll be there Monday morning sharp.

MOLLY: Rosie was making some Easter plans.

GANT: I can't do anything about that. You and she can still have your Easter.

MOLLY: It's the first time in a long while she's made any kind of plans.

GANT: I got work to do, Molly. I'll see you all at lunchtime.

(GANT *exits from screen door.* MOLLY *watches him go then goes to stove and checks the teakettle. She stokes the stove, then goes to the cupboard and gets four bowls. She goes to another cupboard and gets a bottle of vinegar, then fishes around in another cabinet and finds the food coloring.* ROSIE *enters from the hallway in a long flannel nightgown and a housecoat clutched around her.*)

MOLLY: Morning, Rosie.

ROSIE: Molly.

MOLLY: I just put some water on to boil. You want some tea?

ROSIE: Maybe. *(Sits at the table, looks at the bowls, the eggs and the whisky bottle, but does not see any of it.)* I'm not feeling so good.

MOLLY: I figured. You're up a good deal later than usual.

ROSIE: I just couldn't even lift my head off the pillow. I hope Gant got Drew to school on time.

MOLLY: Rosie, look at all the eggs I hardboiled. After you have your tea, we'll color them.

ROSIE: What day is it?

MOLLY: Saturday. The day before Easter.

ROSIE: There ain't no school today.

MOLLY: We've got so much to do today. We got to get ready for that Easter supper we talked about yesterday.

ROSIE: We should have ham for Easter.

MOLLY: Wouldn't ham be nice? I wish we could. I don't remember the last time we had ham.

ROSIE: What's in the pantry? What do we have?

MOLLY: I know we have some beans and corn we canned a couple years back.

ROSIE: It was so hot when we did that canning. For days and days.

MOLLY: It's turned out to be worth it. Lots of people ran out of their canning a long time ago.

ROSIE: We got any fruit canned? We should bake a pie.

MOLLY: I don't know. We might. I still have some brown sugar though, so at least we can bake something. And we can have chicken. We should get

rid of some of those hens that haven't been laying.
They're just using up feed.

ROSIE: You sure?

MOLLY: It'll only be one. We can do with one less hen.

ROSIE: One won't be enough.

MOLLY: One will be fine. *(Checks teakettle)* Water's hot.

ROSIE: I don't think I don't want any tea.

MOLLY: You should have some. Make you feel better.

ROSIE: No. Thank you.

MOLLY: *(Picks up kettle and pours some hot water into bowls)* You want to pour some vinegar in these?

(ROSIE adds vinegar. MOLLY follows with drops of food coloring.)

MOLLY: This will be our yellow bowl, and the blue bowl and the red bowl and let's make a green bowl.

ROSIE: That vinegar is making me a little sick.

MOLLY: I always liked the smell.

ROSIE: It's just not setting right with me.

MOLLY: I'll move it over by the sink. How's that?

ROSIE: No, no just leave them there. I'll be fine.

MOLLY: Let's put an egg in each bowl. Get them started so we can get them finished.

(WILL and GANT enter from screen door.)

MOLLY: I just wanted them, you know. I think they look so pretty all different colors.

WILL: What is that godawful smell?

MOLLY: Vinegar. For the eggs.

(WILL looks into the bowls. GANT goes to the icebox and takes out the bowl of potato salad.)

MOLLY: How's the cow?

WILL: Don't know. Gant thinks it's the feed but I think she should be looked at.

GANT: (*Eating out of the bowl of salad*) Vets don't make free calls.

WILL: It would be cheaper than losing her in the long run.

GANT: Well, none of that means nothing since we don't have any money anyway.

MOLLY: Gant, why don't you sit down and I'll fix you a plate.

GANT: Because I don't want to get any closer to that evil-smelling shit.

MOLLY: I swear! I'll just pack them up and take them on over to our house.

GANT: Now Molly. You don't have to do that.

MOLLY: (*Grabs a cookie sheet and puts bowls on it*) No, the smell is making Rosie sick, and you and Will both have to comment on it. (*Picks up tray and bowl of eggs*) I just thought it would be nice to have colored eggs for Easter. Things have been so turned around here I thought it would be nice to do something the way it's supposed to be done. (*Finds she can't open door, as both hands are full.*)

WILL: Let me help you. (*Tries to take the tray*)

MOLLY: Just get the door for me.

(WILL *does and* MOLLY *exits.*)

GANT: Wonder what's wrong with her.

WILL: I'm not finding out.

GANT: Nobody asked you to. What were you girls talking about?

ROSIE: What?

GANT: You and Molly.

ROSIE: We were just coloring eggs and I didn't feel so good. I still don't.

GANT: What's wrong.

ROSIE: I had one of them headaches this morning. Couldn't lift my head.

GANT: You too, huh?

(WILL *slips out the door and sits on the steps. His departure goes unnoticed.*)

ROSIE: You didn't come to bed last night.

GANT: I didn't quite make it.

ROSIE: I don't sleep good when you're not there. Feels funny. I get cold.

GANT: Rosie. I need for you to do some things for me today.

ROSIE: I should feel better if I lie down for a bit.

GANT: Well, you do that, and when you're feeling better, I'm going to need you to make sure I've got at least two of everything clean and mended—socks shirts, everything.

ROSIE: I know it's clean. I did my laundry twice yesterday.

GANT: That's right. You did.

ROSIE: I'll check it for holes. I can darn socks in bed.

GANT: One more thing. You know where that old duffel is? The one I had in the service?

ROSIE: I believe it's in the big closet off the front room. I can go look.

GANT: I'll go check on it. You just go lie down. Will?

WILL: Yeah? (*Standing and stepping inside*)

GANT: I'll be with you in just a minute.

WILL: We got a lot of things yet to do. (*Sits and leans back*)

GANT: You could go get started on them.

WILL: Nah, I'll just wait for you.

GANT: Come on, Rosie. Let's put you back to bed.

ROSIE: I got to get my wash off the line first.

GANT: Hadn't you ought to get dressed first?

ROSIE: (*Rising and getting basket by door*) Who's going to see me that already hasn't?

GANT: You're absolutely right.

(*She exits.*)

GANT: I just need to hunt something out.

WILL: Go ahead. I'll be here.

(GANT *exits hallway door.* WILL *makes himself very comfortable.* GANT *re-enters some moments later with a duffel over his shoulder and a cardboard box in his arms.*)

WILL: What's that?

GANT: It's for Molly.

WILL: (*Stands and opens box flaps*) For Molly? (*Peers inside, takes an item out*) Gant, these are Drew's baby clothes.

GANT: Give them to Molly.

WILL: I thought you gave all his clothes away.

GANT: I thought we had, too.

WILL: Rosie's gonna—

GANT: I don't want them in the house when I'm away. I don't know why she kept them, but so long as she did, they shouldn't go to waste.

WILL: She'll see them on the baby.

GANT: I'm going to go tell her right now I'm giving them to you. She's apparently been taking them out and looking at them all along.

WILL: You think?

GANT: I don't know. I'll meet you over at your house. (*Exits screen door*)

WILL: (*Watches him go, then picks up the piece of clothing he took out and holds it up. During the speech he will fold it, and close the box up and exit.*) I know that it was a traditional thing to do, but I thought it was cruel and I told Molly so. Molly told me that it was part of Rosie's mourning and if she weren't allowed to wash and dress Drew for that last time she'd feel as though she hadn't properly said goodbye. Gant and I brought him to the kitchen and laid him on the table. That little boy and that big old table. Gant went to the living room while the rest of the search party brought him whisky and talked low. I wasn't being of any use there, so I went back to the kitchen and hauled in a big pan of water. I had to change it three or four times—they couldn't seem to get the dust off of him to Rosie's liking. When he was clean enough and they started to dress him, I helped them to roll him to his side and his mouth fell open. And his mouth was full of dirt, too.

(*It is nighttime and* MOLLY *comes to the screen door with a sweet-potato pie in her hands. She opens the door and comes in quietly. She sets the pie on the kitchen table, and turns to leave as* ROSIE *enters from hallway, dressed in her cotton dress and cardigan.*)

ROSIE: What's this?

MOLLY: What?

ROSIE: (*Pointing at pie on table*) This.

MOLLY: Oh, it's a sweet potato pie for Easter supper. We were out of any fruit in the pantry so it had to be sweet potato.

ROSIE: Sweet potato's fine. With the chicken and all it'll seem more like Thanksgiving, won't it?

MOLLY: I suppose it will.

ROSIE: Is your icebox full?

MOLLY: Pretty full.

ROSIE: I'll just keep it in mine then.

MOLLY: Well, I brought it over so Gant could have some if he wanted it—since he'll be missing supper tomorrow and all.

ROSIE: Yeah.

MOLLY: I was surprised when he told me he was leaving so early, but I suppose he's got to.

ROSIE: It's just going to be you and me then—for supper?

MOLLY: Will should be back by suppertime. Will better be back by suppertime.

ROSIE: You want some coffee? I got some on the stove.

MOLLY: No, thanks. I got a cup getting cold over at our house.

ROSIE: I'm sure Gant will appreciate the pie.

MOLLY: It's not the best one I've ever made.

ROSIE: It's a wonder you could even find all the things to make it with.

MOLLY: I did substitute and scrimp on a thing or two. *(Pause)* Rosie, I don't know how to say this, but I want to thank you for the baby clothes.

ROSIE: *(Unconvincingly)* I meant for you to have them.

MOLLY: I just—we really didn't know how we were going to provide anything like that when the time came.

ROSIE: I'm glad they'll be useful.

MOLLY: We do appreciate them. Well, I guess I'd better get back to my coffee, then off to bed.

ROSIE: Goodnight. See you in the morning.

MOLLY: Goodnight. *(Opens door and starts out)* Oh, do you still want to go to church with me?

ROSIE: How we going to get there?

MOLLY: Oh, no. Will and Gant will have the truck.

ROSIE: If they're not leaving first thing you could ride into town with them and ride back with someone else.

MOLLY: I do want to go.

ROSIE: Doesn't hurt to ask.

MOLLY: Gant down at the shed?

ROSIE: He might be.

MOLLY: I'll just drop by there on my way back. See you in the morning. *(Exits screen door)*

ROSIE: Night.

(ROSIE goes to the icebox and gets a small pitcher of cream, then gets a cup and spoon and sets it all on the table. She pours herself a cup of coffee and sits, with her back to the screen door. GANT enters.)

ROSIE: Did Molly catch up to you?

GANT: Yes, she did. *(Sits at table)*

ROSIE: And?

GANT: We got to leave early. I can't take the chance of missing that train.

ROSIE: You want any coffee?

GANT: I don't think so.

ROSIE: Some of it's real.

GANT: Where'd you get real coffee?

ROSIE: Been saving it.

GANT: What for?

ROSIE: I don't know. Rainy day.

GANT: I guess you've had it for some time.

ROSIE: You want some?

GANT: Yeah. I'll have some.

(ROSIE *gets up, gets cup and pours.*)

GANT: You bake the pie?

ROSIE: No, Molly did. She dropped it by so you could have some since you'll miss supper tomorrow.

GANT: That was nice of her.

ROSIE: You want a piece?

GANT: What kind is it?

ROSIE: Sweet potato.

GANT: I hate sweet potato.

ROSIE: I thought you liked it.

GANT: No. I like pumpkin.

ROSIE: I can't tell the difference.

GANT: I can.

ROSIE: I'll put it in the icebox then so the bugs don't get to it. (*Gets up, picks up pie, looks through her drawers and finds some cheesecloth and wraps the pie*) Why didn't you tell me you were leaving in the morning?

GANT: I did tell you.

ROSIE: No. I'd have remembered.

GANT: I told you the night I signed up.

ROSIE: No. I wouldn't have been making all these Easter supper plans.

GANT: You probably just didn't hear me.

ROSIE: You just didn't tell me. *(Puts pie in icebox. Stands and folds her arms.)*

GANT: Come on, Rosie. Why would I do a thing like that?

ROSIE: You tell me.

GANT: I told you. I know that. I told you when I was leaving and where I was going and why. And none of it has seemed to really make any sense to you. Molly says you've gone on with your plans tomorrow like I was going to be there when you knew I wasn't.

ROSIE: I've known you were going. I packed your socks and shirts and pants and underwear. I packed you a towel and some soap and something to keep you warm. And I knew why I was doing it. I'm not some—

GANT: All right. I didn't mean that.

ROSIE: What did you mean?

GANT: I didn't mean anything. I want—would you sit down for a minute? I can't talk to you when you're standing in the middle of the room.

(ROSIE sits and toys with her coffee spoon.)

GANT: I know that you still get your headaches and all and that sometimes you have to take things slow.

ROSIE: This morning was the first I've had in a long while.

GANT: I know. What I'm saying is with me gone and with Molly having the baby soon, there's going to be a lot more to do around here.

ROSIE: I pull my weight.

GANT: Yes, you do. But you'll have to do that and then some. And you'll have to keep Molly from doing too much.

ROSIE: You know I'd do that anyway. Without having to be told.

GANT: Rosie, this ain't—

ROSIE: I've got a shirt of yours to mend yet. *(Heads toward hallway)*

GANT: Bring it in here so you can finish your coffee. *(Takes a pocketknife out and starts to clean his nails)*

ROSIE: *(Enters with chambray work shirt and sewing box)* You got a big hole in the arm of this. See?

GANT: I caught it on the tractor the other day.

ROSIE: You should have told me. I'd have patched it before I washed it. Hole just got bigger.

GANT: Slipped my mind.

ROSIE: Seems to be happening a lot.

GANT: What?

ROSIE: Things slipping your mind. Like when you'll be leaving.

GANT: Rosie—

ROSIE: And how long you'll be gone.

GANT: There's a reason why I didn't tell you that. It's because I just don't know.

ROSIE: You're just working long enough to pay the loan.

GANT: What if this summer's as bad as the last one? So we pay off the loan but we still don't have anything. No money, no food—nothing. They've got three years worth of work out there—

ROSIE: Three years! Three years!

GANT: I didn't say I was staying out there for three years.

ROSIE: But you didn't say you weren't.

GANT: Would you be—

ROSIE: If this summer's no good and next summer's no good and the next—

GANT: Rosie, would you stop it! Now why do you think I'm doing this? Why? You think I'm doing this to leave my home?

ROSIE: I think there's some truth in that.

GANT: Christ, Rosie! *(Stands and walks around)* I'm doing this so I have a home to come home to...so you have a home and Will and Molly and their child have a home.

ROSIE: So, how long will you be gone?

GANT: I don't know. I just can't say.

ROSIE: It's hard to wait for a day when you're not sure when that day will come.

GANT: I'll be waiting for the day I come home, too.

ROSIE: I suppose that you will. *(Picks up the shirt and looks at it)* I don't think I can just mend this. I'm going to have to patch it.

GANT: Patch it, then.

ROSIE: It's real close to the elbow. I think I've got some denim in here. *(Digs around in box, pulls out denim)* Here it is.

GANT: Your coffee cold?

ROSIE: No, I'm fine. I'll just—oh—

(She has held up the piece of denim to smooth it and cut a piece from it. It is a pair of child's overalls.)

GANT: Oh, Rosie. Please. I'll just tear the shirt again. Leave it.

ROSIE: No. No. *(She has smoothed out the overalls on the table, stroking them, the scissors in hand.)* I can't send you off with holes in your shirt. Can I? *(Begins to hack at overalls with scissors—they aren't cutting.)*

GANT: It's not important—I'll...

ROSIE: *(Hacking away—getting a bit out of control)* The scissors are dull. They just don't want to—

GANT: Rosie.

ROSIE: *(Picking up overalls and trying to tear them)* They won't cut. They won't cut.

GANT: *(Moving toward her)* Rosie, please.

ROSIE: *(Holding overalls to her)* It's your shirt. I need to fix your shirt.

GANT: *(Moves to hold her)* Rosie.

ROSIE: I can't. Oh, God. *(Hugs him back)* I want him back. Damn God, I want him back with us.

GANT: *(Rocking her)* Hush. Hush, now. Hush.

ROSIE: I want my child.

GANT: I want him, too.

ROSIE: I want you to stay.

GANT: I want to stay, Rosie. I wish that I could.

(GANT and ROSIE kiss and hold one another. Arms around each other, they walk into the hallway. The sound of the wind gets louder and the lights slowly brighten. As day breaks, the wind subsides. It is dawn, Easter Sunday. WILL knocks at the back door.)

WILL: Gant? Rosie? You all ain't up.

ROSIE: *(Enters from hall, picks up a kerchief and knocks the dust out of it)* Morning, Will.

WILL: Morning. Happy Easter.

ROSIE: Happy Easter.

WILL: Gant about ready?

ROSIE: He's packed.

WILL: Well, we've got to get going soon. Got a way to go. You got any coffee going?

ROSIE: Last night's on the stove.

WILL: *(Goes over to pot, lifts lid and decides it's O K. Pours some.)* You're about out. *(Drinks some)* This is real. Where'd you get this?

ROSIE: Had it for a while, but there's no more.

WILL: That's a shame.

MOLLY: *(Comes to door with a pan in one hand full of hot cross buns and the bowl of colored eggs in the other)* Happy Easter, Rosie.

ROSIE: Morning, Molly.

MOLLY: I baked some hot cross buns for Easter morning. I hope you haven't had breakfast yet.

ROSIE: None yet.

MOLLY: Good. *(Sets them on the table)* You want me to fix some eggs? I'll fix some.

ROSIE: No. These will be fine.

WILL: Hey, Molly—there's some real coffee on the stove.

MOLLY: No kidding. Where'd you get it?

ROSIE: I'd saved it.

MOLLY: *(Looking into the pot)* Wasn't that smart. Looks to be only a cup or so left. I don't want to take the last of it.

ROSIE: Drink it. I'm not going to save it again.

MOLLY: *(Pours herself a cup)* I'll make a fresh pot. *(Pours out the rest of pot into* WILL's *cup)*

ROSIE: You know where everything is.

MOLLY: Should I make a full pot?

ROSIE: I don't know. I don't want any. Will, you want any?

WILL: Not really. Not after this.

(GANT enters from hallway.)

MOLLY: Gant, you want some coffee?

GANT: Any more of the real coffee?

MOLLY: No.

GANT: No, thanks.

WILL: Here—finish mine—that's the last of it.

GANT: I'll just have some milk.

MOLLY: I don't guess I'll make any coffee.

GANT: *(Seeing the buns on the table)* You bake these, Molly?

MOLLY: Yes. For Easter.

GANT: That's right. *(Goes to icebox, pours a glass of milk, and gets butter)* Hot cross buns for Easter.

(GANT comes to table and sits. ROSIE gets up and gets plates and knives for everyone. Everyone starts passing food.)

MOLLY: I got an Easter bunny this morning.

GANT: All the rabbits that's been around here—how do you know you've got the Easter bunny?

WILL: He told her so.

MOLLY: *(Glares at him)* Well, I haven't seen a rabbit since that last time everyone went out shooting them. I thought we'd got 'em all.

WILL: Not a chance.

MOLLY: So, I step off the back steps this morning and there's a rabbit just sitting there. Wasn't all still, but it didn't look like it wanted to run away either. So I walked over and reached down and picked it up.

GANT: Come on.

WILL: It's true.

GANT: Did it have an egg under it?

MOLLY: Now you're making fun of me.

WILL: She came walking into the house with it under her arm.

MOLLY: He asked if it was for breakfast. I nearly hit him.

GANT: Had to be something wrong with it.

MOLLY: Well there was. It's eyes and ears were just full of dust. Poor thing couldn't see or hear.

ROSIE: *(Drops her knife and it clatters on her plate)* Excuse me.

WILL: I was surprised it didn't smell her. Rabbits have real good sense of smell.

GANT: You keep it, Molly?

MOLLY: I washed it up as much as it would let me and put it in a box in the kitchen. I was going to bring it over to you, Rosie, but I wasn't sure you'd want a rabbit. Even if it is the Easter bunny.

ROSIE: I'm not sure I'd know quite what to do with a rabbit.

GANT: How long you going to keep him?

MOLLY: I don't know—just until he's better, I guess.

WILL: I bet it will be longer than that.

MOLLY: What do I need with a rabbit?

WILL: She's already named him.

GANT: What?

WILL: Guess.

GANT: Not Peter?

MOLLY: Of course I named him Peter, what else are you going to call a rabbit?

WILL: (*Laughing*) Peter Rabbit.

GANT: Or Peter Cottontail?

MOLLY: Go on and laugh. Either of you looked in on Elsie this morning?

WILL: No.

MOLLY: Anyone's got a cow named Elsie doesn't need to make fun of me for naming a rabbit Peter.

GANT: Oh, I should go out and check on her. Late as it is.

WILL: We need to get moving. Molly or Rosie can do that.

GANT: It'll take a minute. Leaving can wait a minute.

ROSIE: Go on. I'll take care of her.

GANT: It will only take a minute.

ROSIE: You need to get going. You'll miss the train.

WILL: Go on, Gant. Get your bag and let's go.

GANT: You put that shirt in?

ROSIE: It's on the bed. I mended it this morning.

(GANT *goes to room to get duffel.*)

MOLLY: I'll clear. (*Gets up and clears the plates, etc.*) You think you'll want something to take with you? Some food?

WILL: Probably. Pack something up.

(ROSIE *gets up and goes out the screen door.*)

MOLLY: Rosie—I'll take care of the cow.

ROSIE: I'm not going to take care of the cow, yet.

MOLLY: *(Sotto voce)* She's been real quiet.

WILL: What did you expect?

MOLLY: I never know.

GANT: *(Returns with duffel)* I'll just go put this in the truck.

WILL: I'm right behind you.

MOLLY: Will, you wait. I'm packing up some food for you. *(She's putting hot cross buns and Easter eggs in a paper bag.)*

WILL: Bring it out.

MOLLY: Will, just wait for it.

(WILL *takes the hint and sits down.)*

(*Focus shift to* ROSIE *and* GANT *outside door.* MOLLY *continues to pack food.)*

GANT: *(Sets duffel down next to him)* Rosie. *(Puts his hands on her arms and turns her to face him)* I will let you know as soon as I can how long I'll be.

ROSIE: Fine.

GANT: It will only be as long as it absolutely has to be. *(Reaches up and takes kerchief off her head)*

ROSIE: Gant, don't, my hair is dirty. *(Reaches for the kerchief that he keeps out of reach)*

GANT: Your hair looks better than this rag on your head.

(GANT *holds it up, then behind him, forcing* ROSIE *to reach around him)*

ROSIE: Gant—cut it out.

GANT: *(She is reaching all the way behind him and he kisses her.)* There—that's all I really wanted.

ROSIE: Sometimes, Gant—can I have my kerchief back now?

GANT: *(Stuffs it in his back pocket)* No.

(WILL and MOLLY come out. WILL's got a paper sack in his hands and MOLLY's got a fistful of eggs in both hands. She tries to put them in the already full bag.)

WILL: Molly, that's enough. That's fine. Leave some for the two of you.

(MOLLY manages to get one handful in, but is left with two eggs in her hand.)

WILL: All set?

GANT: All set.

WILL: *(Kisses MOLLY on the cheek)* All right now. You girls take care of yourselves. I'll be back tonight.

MOLLY: Drive careful. *(Hugs GANT)* We'll be seeing you sooner than you know it.

(The men walk off and the women watch.)

MOLLY: Egg? *(Offers the ones in her hand to ROSIE)*

ROSIE: Sure.

(MOLLY sits on the steps. They roll the eggs between their hands.)

MOLLY: It's true. He'll be back before you know it.

ROSIE: I know.

MOLLY: And maybe with enough money to hold off the bank for a while.

ROSIE: I'm sure he will. *(She starts to walk off.)*

MOLLY: I'll take care of the cow.

ROSIE: Molly, I'll take care of the cow.

MOLLY: You should go over and have a look at my Easter bunny.

ROSIE: I will as soon as I take care of the cow.

MOLLY: I'll get started on the supper then.

ROSIE: You've already done all the baking. I don't know what you've got left to do.

MOLLY: The chicken. I've got to take care of the chicken.

ROSIE: Will won't be back until after dark. It can wait.

MOLLY: Well, I just thought...

ROSIE: God in heaven, Molly! Will you just sit still for five minutes and eat your egg.

(ROSIE *exits toward direction of shed.*)

(MOLLY *sits and peels her egg.*)

MOLLY: It seemed at times like things was all coming to an end. That there wasn't going to be a hole to crawl out of when it was all said and done. If it wasn't the blow it was the storms the land couldn't soak up. And then the floods. And the grasshoppers. And the land burning. So much gone that what was left hardly looked like a place a person could call home. A lot of people thought it was their fault—their punishment for one thing or another. I don't know. What could folks do that would be so bad they'd deserve this? I couldn't imagine. Well, I never believed we were being punished—maybe measured—just to see how we'd stand up to it all. That seemed more like it. And I never believed I'd never see good weather again. I never believed we wouldn't see things growing here again. But a lot of people never believed. And they left. Sure, there was a point where even I thought things couldn't get any worse. Then it did get worse. Again and again.

But after a while there wasn't nothing left that could surprise us. And that was the beauty of it all.

(MOLLY *bites into her egg and the lights fade to black.*)

END OF PLAY